Past Imperfect

New & Selected Poems

Neil Silberblatt

Nixes Mate Books
Allston, Massachusetts

ISBN 978-1-949279-03-0

Nixes Mate Books
POBox 1179
Allston, MA 02134
nixesmate.pub/books

… We must have
the stubbornness to accept our gladness in the ruthless
furnace of this world. To make injustice the only
measure of our attention is to praise the Devil.
If the locomotive of the Lord runs us down,
we should give thanks that the end had magnitude.
– from *A Brief for the Defense*, by Jack Gilbert (1925 – 2012)

for Max & Zoe,
my greatest poems

for Chev,
with gratitude undimmed &
love unbroken

Contents

Past Imperfect

New & Selected Poems

Breathe (CT Scan)

Hold your breath.
Yes, but where precisely?
The gown offers no pockets
for such things,
and the locker
has little room.

Breathe.

Hold your breath.
Until when exactly?
Until the cancer retreats or advances,
or lays in wait
like guerrillas under Che
for the right moment?

Breathe.

Hold your breath.
But in which hand, pray tell?
I'm a southpaw.
But something so precious
should be clasped with both,

lest it slip out.

Breathe.

Hold your breath.

Fine, I'm holding.
Still holding.

Exodus

Thanks to the wonders of chemotherapy,
my hair is leaving my scalp
first, in small familial strands
then, en masse.
The way whites fled Queens
for the island of Long.
The way Jews fled Egypt and Russia
and then Bushwick and Bensonhurst.

What once rested on my head,
between skull and skull cap,
now rests in my shower drain
resembling nothing so much
as a drowned vole,
mocking my vanity and array
of hair care products.

Perhaps, like those of my tribe,
my hair will change its name,
get a dye job and migrate
strand by strand
to a new promised land.

Or, perhaps, after a period of desolation
and abandoned landscapes,
marked by depreciating values,
it will return
finer and thinner than before.
Just look at Williamsburg.

Prick

Let me know if you feel this
Prick
as she perforates my hands and feet with a
Prick
driving slender needles into them
like some gentler crucifixion,
careful to leave no stigmata.

With each
Prick
I recall my zafta,
her hands like worn baseball mitts
creased and broken in,
inserting needles into her tomato shaped
pincushion, lest she
Prick
those blessed fingers reserved
for baking challah and pinching cheeks.

Let me know if this
Prick
restores feeling to your hands or feet
stolen by that
Prick

Oxaliplatin,
its name reminiscent of some
sadistic Roman
Prick.

Tell me if this
Prick
in the center of your skull
erases the memory of that
Prick
who tormented you daily, calling you "faggot"
because you couldn't hit or throw a ball straight
And how you wanted so badly to call him
Prick
except you knew that his fist
ached for an excuse.

Tell me if this
Pricks
your conscience and eases
the premonition of death which
Pricks
at you like a thorn
or, perhaps, something more than a
Prick
is required.

In the Bullpen at Dana Farber

Waiting in the pen at
Dana Farber, a fly ball from
Fenway, getting ready for his turn
at the Green Monster, he tells me
unprompted
of the woman to whom
he was wed for 70 years.

How she made a home to which
he looked forward to returning,
which he no longer calls home.
How she wanted so badly to make it
to their youngest daughter's wedding.
How she succeeded.
How she slipped away the day after.

Accompanied by his adult daughter,
who squeezes his arm as though
he were a pump and her hand a blood-pressure cuff,
he tells me of his mother who
raised six children
after his father died, too young.

Cleaning his thin-framed glasses which
have become streaked,
and weaving his fingers through his daughter's,
he tells me of the parachute which
saved his life when he was shot down
over Australia, and how,
at war's end, he returned home with that silk
from which his wife made a baptismal gown for his
children and their children,
as his daughter extricates her hand from his
and cleans her now streaked glasses.

And, somehow, the subject
of his advanced pancreatic cancer
never comes up before he is
called to swing for the fences.

Final Requests

When it's my turn
at bat, skip the cremation.
Enough of my tribe have been shoved into ovens.
No need to add my meager ration.

Instead, roast me like coffee
till my bones attain a darker hue,
like my beloved.
Then measure out my days
into a French press,
where you can label me robust, complex and,
at long last, rich.

Or, once the Angel of Death has koshered me –
as my zeyde did to chickens and goats – never calves
whose eyes, he said, were too much like a child's –
giving thanks to the Almighty with each gentle
stroke of his sharp blade –

Cook me, slowly, over a low flame
as my mother did with flanken –

starting on early Friday afternoon
so it would be ready in time for Shabbos
until the meat fell off the bone with a glance –

Then, perhaps, those who are curious
or maybe hungry, can see and taste
how a poet burns.

Kashrut

To keep kosher, you must separate
the milk from meat,
the pure from the impure,
the sacred from the profane.

You must segregate the food,
herd the designated and ritually slaughtered animals
into their refrigerated ghettos
where they cannot be contaminated
by contact with the unclean.

To keep kosher, you must draw
the blade against the jugular,
quickly and with a single stroke,
let it bleed out and cook each to its own.

You must boil the spoon or fork
which has landed briefly in the wrong drawer, or
bury the plate which has borne
the forbidden in the earth, where it can absorb
the ashes from the
remains of the kosher.

You must be prepared to discard the impure
to slaughter your second born
to banish your first born
to claim your brother's birthright
to deceive your elderly half-blind father
to bury your brother and leave him for dead
to bear suffering with Bontshe Shveig-like silence
and to wait three hours between devouring the kid
and drinking its milk.

You must renounce all manner of shellfish
and your brother and his children if they transgress
and stand silent as they are swallowed by the earth.

Above all, you must purify your soul
soaking it in brine for the requisite millennia
until it hardens, before roasting
and hope that, when you are done,
it is pleasing to god
and his people.

The Plagues, as Recalled by a Former Slave

The first one
frogs, I think.
It's been a while – and there was all that wandering.
Never seen so many.
And, of course, we had to get rid of them,
come morning.

Then, they came faster.
Blood, thick, like the Euphrates was menstruating.
Boils, as though you'd been sprayed by hot grease.
And we had to wipe up all that blood
and soothe all those blisters,
come morning.

I remember the last one clearly, though.
The midnight howls of our masters
watching their eldest boys drop like those locusts,
some still asleep in their cribs.
We recognized that howl.
We knew its dimensions.

Not for us this slaughter.
We never prayed for that
kind of revenge.
But we knew who they'd be coming after,
come morning.

How to Build a Fire (for Chev)

Start slowly,
no, slower
with longing or, perhaps,
a lemon cut along its pregnant midsection and
squeezed over plump scallops seared to a walnut
finish while their flesh recalls the ocean.

Nurse it with desire or, perhaps,
garlic roasted until its sweet pulp emerges
Minerva-like from its parchment skin, like Torah scrolls
whose crowned letters leap from flames.

Only then, add touch or, perhaps,
logs whose air pockets wait to be emptied
by pickpocket flames, releasing ash fireflies
like so many copper pennies scattered onto
the night's floor.

Skip the fire pit.
You don't even need matches.
Just start with kindling or, perhaps,
a poem about kindling.

Family Portraits

I.　*Scenes from a Marriage*

In the beginning, when we had the place to
ourselves, it was good we said
parroting his words.
Before the flood, before the fall.
Before the children who changed all.

Yes, there were fights.
Before we had words, we would grunt and
scream sure that no one would hear us.
I offered to leave once, gesturing to the gate.
Wordlessly, she begged me to stay and
make this garden grow.

In time, the battles – like the garden and
her belly, both cultivated – bloomed.
Familiarity bred contempt
and poisoned fruit polluted this eden.

After the tragedy, of which we no longer
speak except in mumbled glances or silent
quickly-retracted neverminds,

we moved on from place
to unremembered place

which were never as good
as at the beginning.

II.   *Answer Pending*

He never did get an answer.
When Cain was facing eviction
and asked the absentee landlord
that question about brothers,
he did not stick around
long enough
for a reply.

Just packed his bags,
gassed up the car,
and left town
with that question
and that mark.

III.   *The Other Woman*

She could hear them going at it
in the next room,
with his labored breathing
and hers, bearing his weight with each thrust,
waiting for them to finish,
for him to return to her bed.

They did not even pay her the honor of
subterfuge or silence, which she had been
promised when she offered him this woman.

She could not object. She could not demand
that he pull his body off, or out of, hers.
This other woman – so despised for her
still supple skin,
her breasts still filled with milk,
but most for her unpardonable otherness -
was, after all, the mother of his first born.
A son who – with every glance, gesture, shout –
reminded her so much of him
and her own fruitless womb.

Nonetheless, the sound of his ancient heaving
grunting body seeking and
finding refuge in hers, filled her
with a rage which nurtured her
and her not yet conceived child,
as though they could both suckle on it.

When, at last, a child grew in her own aged body
after bearing the child, the whispered derision
the well-meaning but cruel questions
            how old is your grandson?
she ordered the other woman banished
together with the other's child,
his first-born son,
who would grow up to remember and
avenge his father's kindness.

IV.   The Main Event

"… So Jacob was left alone, and a man wrestled with him till daybreak."
    Genesis 32:24

Gentlemen, you know the rules.
I want a good, clean fight.
No rabbit punches.
No kidney punches.
No graven images.
No blows below the belt.
No invoking my name or
biting or scratching.
No gouging of eyes or
beating of wings.
No glimpses of mortality.
No slaying of the first born.
 1 2 rounds, regulation match.

The winner will be by TKO
and – in addition to the usual prize money –
will receive a new name and set of luggage
good for a millennia of wandering.

Shake hands.
Go to your tents.
Come out fighting.

V.   *When He Left*

When he left her, she would feel his warm breath
on her cheek before his bristled hair tickled her awake,
before her lips found his in the still dark.

She would be left behind, always
behind to take care of the children,
to tend wounds, ease tears, coax laughter
if laughter would come,
to wait for his return or the message
that something had happened, and then
with tear-stained voice, to explain
if explanation would come.

She understood that she was not his first or last
love mattered little to such a man,
though he had his share, no doubt
that the voice which resonated in his ear,
but never spoke to her,
would not let him rest
by her side. Still.

When he left, she missed the warmth of
his body, his breath falling against her skin
like a dense fog, and ached for his safe
return from Pharaoh's temple
in Memphis.

In the end, it was never just
the bush which burned
without being consumed.

VI.   Protocol

No, no, no. This is not how you bear
such news. You carry this as you might
carry an infant, depositing it gently into
the right arms. There is a protocol to
such things as in knowing precisely when
to rend garments and how the rending is
to be done. No whispered message
that he is no more.

You must approach cautiously
your eyes attentive, as though you
were joining a panther clawing at the ground,
lest he tear at the throat which carries such words.

You must practice your speech, choosing
your words as carefully as his murderer
chose his weapon.

And you cannot leave him there. Alone.
His flesh, as smooth and comely and warm
as a woman's,
is now pallid and pierced
and coldening.

Bring him inside,
where my rage and grief
can keep him warm.

VII.   Lazarus, or Second Acts

"Now a certain man was sick, Lazarus of Bethany … So when [Jesus]
heard that he was sick, He then stayed two days longer in the place
where He was …"

>   *The Gospel of John 11:1–6.*

For starters, Lazarus was not sick.
He was dead.
For four days,
and beginning to smell.

And why him?
When none else
merited a second turn.
Not the other John,

whose restless body
ached to be re-attached
to his resting head.
He was left in twain.

Not his step-dad,
who endured the mockery

and murmuring glances,
cuckolded, it was whispered, by god.

Not even his mom,
who held his body,
as she had nursed him,
his lips pressed to her breast.

And what words did he say
as he breathed life into
this rotting corpse? Perhaps nothing
more than I would whisper to you now.
"Oh, won't you stay
Just a little bit longer.
Please let me hear you
say that you will."

VIII.   John the Baptist (after Rodin)

He stands there –
forever outside the Gates of Paradise -
lips parted
hair flowing
buck naked.

Right index finger raised -
as though about to point out
something or other.
Left index finger pointing
at his well-muscled calf,
advancing toward the viewer,
head still attached.

Since the subject was unavailable,
one wonders as to the model.
Supposedly, an Italian peasant from Abruzzi –
Pignatelli, of whom little is known –
to whom the sculptor
perhaps offered a free meal or drink,
which might explain the raised
index finger
and parted lips.

Looking at him now – still, muscled
but in restless motion -
I wait for him to walk towards me.
To receive his benediction.
To share his certainty.

No wonder she wanted his head.
Who could resist those lips?

IX.   *Mother's Day*

After the muslin was removed
from the mirrors and her shoulders,
she returned the wooden benches,
which she used when she sat for her husband
and now would see no further service,
and waited so patiently
for his return.

Every noise, every stirring of wind
would stir her awake,
certain that it was he.
But the wind was
simply the wind,
carrying nothing but stale air
moved about.

She heard, by rumor, that he had visited the others
and that woman,
invited them to examine his wounds,
see for themselves,
a little show and tell,
even had dinner with them.
But not her.

She did not need to see the stigmata,
feel the viscera,
touch the space left by the spear.
She had seen and touched
enough of his wounds
from when he first skinned his knee.
She needed no more.

Just to hear his voice again
once
before muslin was draped over her
would have sufficed.

X. Vidui (Confession)

Ashamnu.[1]
Bagadnu.[2]
Ta'inu.[3]

No, I never visited her.
Never comforted her in her days of shiva.
After that Friday, we did not speak again.

Should I have apologized for putting her
through all that?
Making her wait during the years
of wandering, only to force her to watch
her only child be tormented?
To bear a child, and then bear his body?
How could I have explained?

She would have entreated me to stay,
to make her a grandmother,
to look after her in old age,

---

1   *We have been guilty.*
2   *We have betrayed.*
3   *We have gone astray.*

to be by her withered hand
as her weathered mind wandered.

"Who else?", she would have asked.
"You are the last of my line."

She would have begged me, if only to say
Kaddish for her and place a rock on her stone.
That was a cross I could not bear.
Better, I should not speak with her again.
I see the Rabbi here for atonement.
I tell him I have reserved a suite
of rooms for her
in my father's house.

V'all kulam, alohei slihot.
S'lach lanu.
M'chal lanu.
Kaper lanu.[4]

---

4   *For all of these, God of compassion. Forgive us, pardon us, grant us*
     atonement.

Instructions from My 94 Year Old Mother

If I forget to
take my medicine, lose
my thought or misplace
my keys or who you are,
give me a clue
like in charades
or leave post-it notes on the fridge
where I will be sure to see them,
if I remember to look.

If I forget my
appointment or the year, or nod
off, rouse me with nettles
boiled and sterilized
no, not nettles
you know, but you won't tell me, will you
needles, that's it
not the ones for knitting
the other ones.

If I forget my
gloves or thoughts
which have loosened themselves

again and fallen off one by
one, waiting to be gathered
for lost and found
re-attach them
with soft words and post-it notes.
And why do you talk of nettles?

The Armband (April 5, 1968)

Since you asked,
it's a cotton/poly blend.
60/40, I believe, to avoid shrinkage.
The fabric is textured to enhance
the wave of the skirt (for which it was intended).
The color?
You could call it black,
but that would show an appalling
lack of imagination,
since there are so many shades of black.
From ebony to onyx.
From Lena Horne to Nina Simone.
This one is called "midnight".
You may see it this fall
on the ivory mannequins or customers
at B. Altman's or Macy's
or, two years from now,
in bags of darker skinned shoppers
at S. Klein or May's.

But, I said none of this
that morning on the schoolhouse steps
when asked about the armband I had fashioned

from stolen fabric, borrowed courage and pinking shears
the day after his murder in Memphis.
Or when commanded by the principal,
who mocked my stutter and tears,
to re- re- re- remove it.
One of the many commandments I ignored,
my 10-year old body shaking with shame and rage,
all the way home.

High, Dry & Near a Racetrack

Dad, I have gotten lost again
on my way to you and mom.
I know how you valued punctuality
placing it among the cardinal virtues.
But, I'm afraid I'll be late
though not as late as you.

Navigating through freshly dug mounds
and neglected headstones,
I pass the black-hatted Greek choruses
who guide the bereaved through their rounds
of mourning and rock in place
as they recite prayers for strangers.

This landscape resists
any cartographer, but is so familiar
and welcoming, with streets named
after patriarchs and prophets,
and the scent of horses and sweet hay.

There you are
waiting for me,
with mom in her still unmade bed.

Your stony silence suits you.
You were never one for
small talk or words left unsaid.

So, let me begin the conversation
with a rock for your stone.
Your turn.

Butternut Squash Atonement – A Recipe

In the beginning was the Word,
and the Word was
butter – unsalted, cream butter -
not Fleishman's or Imperial,
not "I can't believe" – although
I don't
any longer.
Just enough to hide the wrapper
from my mom,
who would ask,
who – in her 95 years – never ate milk with meat.
Knowingly.

Into this sinful butter
is cast chopped celery and onions
and whole garlic cloves (2 or 3),
cooked until the celery is soft,
the onion translucent,
and the mixture smells of home.

Now, chicken stock is added (4 cups).
Kosher for my mom,
who would ask,

who – in her 95 years – never ate non-Kosher meat
lest her entry be barred in Gan Ayden.[5]

Into this comes butternut or winter squash
roasted until smooth and mashed
until resembling the color of
the clay of her Kishinev shtetl.

Then, savory and rosemary –
burlesque strippers –
who tease the flavor out of this soup.

At the very end, cream is added.
Non-dairy, for my mom,
who would ask,
and fresh-grated nutmeg.

Once, by mistake, I used real cream
and lied to her.
How she loved the taste of that soup.
How she forgave the lie,
asking for seconds.

---

5   *Gan Ayden – Hebrew for Garden of Eden (Paradise).*

Oh, do not cast her from Paradise
on account of that tainted soup.
Let the sin be on me
and the sweet taste be on her lips
for eternity.

Aisle 14

For the moment, they rest here in the cool mist.
Figs from Lebanon in close embrace with dates

from Syria – keeping watchful eye on
thin-skinned Jaffa oranges.

Korean kimchi in forced peaceful coexistence
with Russian beluga, laid out in icy splendor,

recalling days cohabiting in the bellies of sturgeon
swimming in contested waters.

Olives in military camouflage, harvested in Ramallah,
bulldozed over to make room for settlements,

share space with blood-red pomegranates
culled from collective farms in Judea

fertilized in an uneasy truce
with rockets imported from Gaza.

Stand Your Ground

Stand your ground
like a tree that's planted by the water,
near the banks of the North Canadian River
this clear day in May,
as you jostle with others
for a good spot
to take pictures
of Laura and her 15-year old boy Lawrence
hanging from the bridge
like strange fruit.

Stand your ground
by the large sycamore tree
near City Hall in Waco
on another day in May,
as 17 year old Jesse,
his body muscled from hauling bales of hay
now naked and beaten,
baptized in coal oil,
hoisted like a flag
by his neck and lowered into the fire,
as the flames lick his skin
and his wordless screams fill the
smoke-filled spring sky.

Stand your ground
near the noisy fairgrounds by the silent railyard
as young Henry
is placed upon a scaffold,
ten feet high,
and his body is caressed
by red hot iron brands
as kerosene is poured upon him,
and set alight,
as little ones eat fried dough
and wave banners.

Stand your ground
along an asphalt road
this dark night in June,
as James, his feet bound -
like a latter-day Saint Sebastian -
is driven across the back roads of Jasper
greeting every rock
every stone
until his body gives out.

Stand your ground
for this child,
his skin the color of
        the soil of those river banks
        the bark of that sycamore
        the lumber of that kerosene-soaked scaffold
        the dirt of that Jasper road
has not been the first
who has been laid low
for no reason.

Stand your ground
though it quakes
though it opens beneath you
though it threatens to swallow you whole.

Stand your ground,
like a tree that's planted by the water;
you shall not,
no, you shall not be moved.

Why I Stopped Smoking (for Eric Garner)

Among the warnings on the side
of the pack or carton, next to the dire
but unheeded prophecies to you and your
unborn children, should be this
emblazoned with skull and crossbones.

CAUTION

If you sell these on a street
corner in Staten Island,
and they are loose
and you are black,
there is a very real danger of your
being choked to death.
It really is a filthy habit.
Quit now.

A Picture is Worth

In the photo
taken at the County Courthouse
in Tallahatchie, Mississippi
in September 1955
the Eisenhower days of drive ins and Buddy Holly
Bobby Soxers and all white counters,
she is a fairly attractive woman
with stenciled eyebrows
not unlike my mom's
and cute bobbed hair with an errant
cow lick she could not suppress.

In the photo
taken at the County Courthouse
she has a tapered face that Modigliani would admire
or that Thomas Hart Benton could do justice to
with her two young sons close by
in outfits she must have picked out for the occasion
matching short-sleeve white shirts
suspenders, jeans
fresh haircuts
the younger one seated on her lap
all gazing unsmiling into the camera.

In the photo
taken at the County Courthouse
she and her boys are seated in the front row
before an audience
all white
could be a church gathering
were it not a murder trial.
An old man – out of a Norman Rockwell -
is smiling toothlessly just over her older son's head.

In the photo
taken at the County courthouse
you cannot hear her perjured testimony
given after she placed her hand on that Bible
before her two boys
and God
and the good State of Mississippi
that this man
this Black man from Chicago
who was only 14 years old
seven years younger than she
had leered at her
grabbed at her
said he had done *something* with white women.
Something – the word left to foul the air

like a beaten and bloated corpse –
the all white audience
would surely understand.

In the photo
taken at Roberts Temple Church of God in Christ
in Chicago, Illinois
in September 1955
through glass-sealed casket
so all could see what was done to her boy
by that attractive woman's husband and his brother
Emmett is also wearing clothing
his mom picked out for the occasion
fresh white shirt
dark suit
crewcut of what was left of his singed hair.
But his 14 year old mummified face
is unrecognizable as a face.
It is a torn and battered canvas
where a face once was.
It is not a face for painters,
or for poets.

Wood

I.

The swing is different,
smoother, the wood ones
make a nice swoosh, solid
pine, with the logo burned into the grain
and Powerized with double lightning bolts.
You line up both fists under the L in Louisville
and get a nice thwack if you hit it just
right like Big Papi with that shit-eating grin.
Not like aluminum, where you get a
ping. Aluminum, that's for beer or siding or
gates they slide down and lock when they
don't want us looking in after
they're closed because we might
take our bats and aim for their home plate
glass windows, just to get a nice cold one,
please.

II.

You want to be careful with that, and don't be
pointing at anything you don't want to kill.

They made them out of wood a long
time ago. My uncle had a rifle with a buttstock
out of walnut, which he stroked before aiming
at some bird or deer, squeezing one off.
He'd show me where to aim for best result.
Best, unless you were the bird or deer.
This one here is made from hardened nylon.
Smooth as stockings, gets off 17 rounds just like
that, but it sounds different going into bone.
Wood splits or cracks under pressure.
Bullets, they do what they're supposed
into hide, feather or bone.
They don't know, they just
don't.

III.

Care, that's what the nice man said
eyes and voice lowered and hands clasped,
as though his left was comforting his right.
Care for the deceased – they don't say corpse –
they never say corpse – and next of kin. He showed us
two kinds, solid oak or mahogany, depending on how
much we could afford to
care and – well we're not

going to spend it on college now – so we went with
mahogany and cream colored satin inside.
Looking at him resting there, all nice in a suit and
patched up as best they could,
I want to scream
"That's my boy, my son. They murdered him."
I want to hear someone say
"We're all full up. No more room in the ground
for black boys cut down like August corn.
Let them grow a bit. Let their hair
whiten."
I want my howls
to wake him from that cream colored bed. Like when
God returned Job's kids and said all's okay
now.
Just testing.
Give me back my son or at least,
let me take his place.
I don't want to curse, I don't,
but he was my only and that
man had no cause, no sir, none at all, to
Shoot.

Be Kind, Rewind

That day,
that cloudless Tuesday,
with its Chartres-blue sky,
I could not watch the news.

Instead, I taped the broadcasts
for later watching.

That night,
that quiet night
marred only by the ululation of widows,
I re-wound the tape and watched in reverse
as towers rose from toxic dust
as windows formed from shards of glass and
micrograms of mercury oxide
as confettied papers re-assembled themselves into
binders and file cabinets
and as young men
spread eagled like Icarus
      in casual business attire,
            ascended on plumes of ash
                  against the Chartres-blue sky
                     and reached their offices,

just in time
for that all important

1 0: 1 5 conference call.

Kingdom of Heaven

My ex-husband tells me that I am no longer
a good Christian and cannot enter the kingdom of

heaven, or our former marital home, the
locks to both having been changed, now

that our divorce is final, placing my soul
in jeopardy along with my once immaculate

credit rating. And it's good to know he's concerned
about such things, and would he mind

changing the outgoing message on the home
answering machine, since it may tend to confuse Jesus.

On the Yahrzeit of Ezra Pound

I cannot bring myself to light a candle
for the bastard, as brilliant as he was and,
besides, he would not want my
circumcised prayers in that guttural tongue.

Do his goose-stepping friends deserve a Kaddish?
Perhaps Eichmann merits a novena over his ashes
forever enshrined in the cool Mediterranean.

After all, the butchers are in need of prayers
far more than the butchered. The souls of incinerated
children do not require our intercession. Once baked,
they will pass nicely from ovens into paradise,
bypassing poets fluent in Greek.

Or would the words halt en route after
they had passed over my diseased Kike tongue
and decline to go farther, refusing a direct order
unlike a good German.

No, this is the best revenge.
I will squeeze them out
like a kidney stone. He would have hated the

sanctimonious forgiveness of it.
Confutatis maledictis,
Flammis acribus addictis.
Voca te cum benedictis.[6]
Yisgadal, v'yiskadash.

6   Once the cursed have been rebuked,
sentenced to acrid flames.
Call thou you with the blessed.

For Madiba

Our heroes were not allowed
to ripen into patinaed old age.
Like fiddlehead ferns or spring lamb, they were
harvested early while still young, tender
cut down in motorcades or grand ballrooms
or on cheap hotel balconies.
We were left to imagine what havoc
age might wreak on their soft faces or hard ideals.

He was the exception.
Improbably, he ripened before us
surviving almost three decades behind bars
hair whitening, once boyish cheeks gaining,
then losing their fur.
Outlasting a brutal regime which kept him
alive for sport or, more likely, for fear
of the pale heads which would blossom
on pikes after his murder.
Refusing his daily bread and forgiving his trespassers
as we could not hope to forgive those
who trespass against us.

Soft make his room now with broad vistas
and no walls.
From the soil of Soweto he was made, and
into its sweet welcoming bosom,
he returns.

Saint Francis

It must have been the hat.
On those early album covers,
before I unsheathed your shining vinyl,
careful not to place my fingers on your grooves,
you were always wearing a hat
with silk ribbon above the brim
or grey borsalino
smooth and half-cocked, like you.
And you offered dispensation for us sinners,
and one more for my baby,
now and at the wee small hour of our despair.

When you gave up the hat,
you lost me.
In '74, you tried again with another hat
but it was a cartoonish thing
perched on your head
and your voice was gone.
And I was ashamed for you.

But what do you know
of love or loss?
You let Ava Gardner go
and danced with Nancy Reagan.

The Visit (for Joe G.)

When I entered, the door and your lips
were both ajar,
parted slightly to let others
know you were still breathing
as they silently reviewed your vitals,
not as vital as they once were.
I did not call before coming,
certain that you would say not to bother
certain that I would ignore you
certain of little else.
As you slept, I stole one of the errant
grapes from your tray table
as it rolled closer to the lime green
sugar free jello, so tepid and so tasteless,
glancing at your well-balanced meal
and you
both going to waste.
I wanted to rub your hands
or a rosary, but
did not know which knuckle or bead
represented grace
and which
the hour of our parting.

Chicago

Being in love, she says,
her voice heavy with Dilaudid,
is like being in Chicago.
And I smile, having been
in Chicago and
felt the winds whip off Lake Michigan
down Wells Street,
cutting to the bone
no matter how many layers,
taking your breath away,
knocking you off your feet,
bringing you to tears,
leaving you craving another's warmth.
And, Dilaudid or no,
her directions are spot on.

Autobiography

These lines,
begun in earnest good hope
and great expectations,
have been severely edited.
Cut to pieces.
Ripped to shreds.
Whole sections -
which seemed perfectly fine
at the time -
scrapped entirely
by a merciless editor.

These lines
have grown so weary
of being perused and picked at
like scabs.
They just want to be left
alone to enjoy the warmth
of your hands and cloth-bound covers,
like their author.

Acknowledgments

"In the Bullpen at Dana Farber" and "How to Build a Fire" – *Muddy River Poetry Review* (Fall 2017).

"Kashrut, The Other Woman" and "On the Yahrzeit of Ezra Pound" – *Poetica Magazine* (Spring 2015).

"Mother's Day" – *Oddball Magazine* (May 2014).

"Instructions from My 94 Year Old Mother" – *Canopic Jar* (December 2017).

"Aisle 14" – *Arc-24 Literary Review* (December 2015).

"Stand Your Ground" – *Verse Wisconsin* (Fall 2012).

"Why I Stopped Smoking" – *Split this Rock* (December 2014).

"Be Kind, Rewind" – *Nixes Mate Review* (Fall 2017).

"The Visit" – *PrimeTime Cape Cod* (March 2016).

"Autobiography" – *The Aurorean* (Spring/Summer 2018).

"Butternut Squash Atonement" will be published in the anthology *Culinary Poems* (Glass Lyre Press).

About the Author

Neil Silberblatt's poems have appeared in numerous journals, including *Poetica Magazine, The Aurorean, Two Bridges Review, Ibbetson Street Press, Naugatuck River Review, Chantarelle's Notebook, Canopic Jar, First Literary Review, Muddy River Poetry Review, Nixes Mate Review*, and *The Good Men Project*. His work has also been, or will soon be, published in various anthologies, including *Confluencia in the Valley: The First Five Years of Converging with Words* (Naugatuck Valley Community College, 2013); University of Connecticut's *Teacher-Writer* magazine; *Collateral Damage* (Pirene's Fountain); and *Culinary Poems* (Glass Lyre Press). He has published two poetry collections: *So Far, So Good* (2012), and *Present Tense* (2013), and has been nominated for a Pushcart Prize. Neil is also the founder/director of Voices of Poetry which, since 2012, has organized and presented a series of poetry events (featuring acclaimed poets) at various venues in NY, NJ, CT and MA. He is also the host of the Poet's Corner program on WOMR/WFMR out of Provincetown, MA.

42° 19′ 47.9″ N   70° 56′ 43.9″ W

Nixes Mate is a navigational hazard in Boston Harbor used during the colonial period to gibbet and hang pirates and mutineers.

Nixes Mate Books features small-batch artisanal literature, created by writers who use all 26 letters of the alphabet and then some, honing their craft the time-honored way: one line at a time.

nixesmate.pub/books

CPSIA information can be obtained
at www.ICGtesting.com
Printed in the USA
LVHW081748070120
642794LV00016B/1487/P